MW01101599

ReDiscover Church: Ten Reasons Why People Leave and Why They're Coming Back

Outreach, Inc., Vista, CA 92081

www.outreach.com

ISBN: 978-0-9823744-2-9

Author: Kim Levings, Vice President, Outreach, Inc.
Cover and Interior Design: Alexia Wuerdeman

Printed in the United States of America

TABLE OF CONTENTS

IF YOU'VE OPENED THIS BOOK...

YOU PROBABLY WANT to see if we've included *your* reason for not going to church anymore. We hope so, and we also hope, too, that you will reDiscover church after reading our responses to each of the reasons why people leave the church.

To put your mind at rest, here are just a few points to consider before you start reading:

This book is *not*:

- Going to judge you or make you feel guilty about leaving the church.
- Intended to force you into any change of heart or decision to go back to church.
- An easy "what to do" in terms of your life situation–that's personal and unique to you.

This book *is*:

- A review of common reasons people leave the church.
- An honest and realistic response to each of these reasons.
- Intended to get you thinking again–and possibly give you a new awareness of what you might be missing without an active church life.

So give in to your urge, and jump straight to the reason that most resonates with your personal "church" story. Then take the time to review the other sections –you may find some nuggets in each of them that are helpful to you.

If this book is useful to you, tell the person who gave it to you, and consider passing it on to someone else. Of course, we really do hope you think about coming back. This could be an important moment in your life.

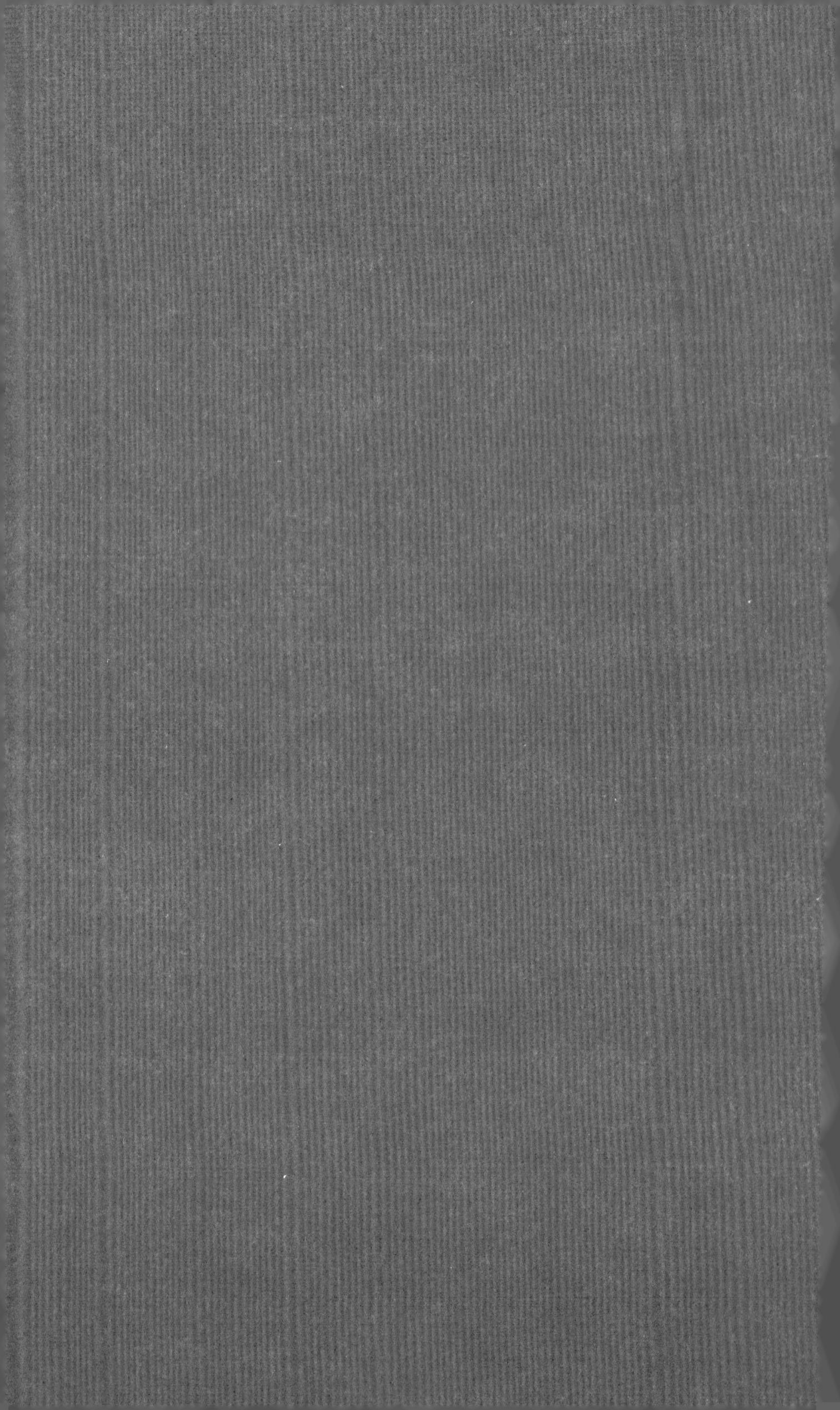

REASON #1:

I DON'T BELIEVE IN ORGANIZED RELIGION.

POPULAR CULTURE IS full of loose terms. Many people throw out "organized religion" without much thought. What exactly is "organized religion"? Perhaps it means that a governing body of sorts–a group of leaders or rulers–unilaterally determines what is and isn't right for people. Or, maybe your understanding of the term is related to previous experience of denominational culture, the different way "things are done" by Methodists, Presbyterians, Catholics, Baptists, and many more.

> *"We need God, not in order to understand the why, but in order to feel and sustain the ultimate wherefore, to give a meaning to the universe."*
>
> –MIGUEL DE UNAMUNO (1864-1936)

Let's dig a little deeper into the term "organized religion" itself. Trouble is, church by its very nature *has* to be organized. "Religion" is the real issue. In fact, Jesus spent more time rebuking the Pharisees on this topic than anything else. The Pharisees were the "organized religion" of that time, and they had made it all about rules and dos and don'ts at the expense of a realistic understanding of the love of God. (Yeah, I bet you still know some of them, right?)

The church of today still has its share of Pharisees. It's sad, but true. Just like in government, you will always have somebody in every church that is too conservative, too rigid, and resistant to change. You've probably even worked with people who have a "my way or the highway" mindset–and of course, you are always on their wrong side, because you don't measure up to their definition of what you're supposed to say, do, or be!

"Organized" religion is not really what it's about; discovering God and meeting Him in the person of Jesus is what it's about. Sometimes this means rising above a few Pharisees you meet along the way.

So, what would dis-organized religion look like, anyway? "Anything goes!" "Hey, buddy, if it feels right, it must be OK, right?" "Any way you choose is OK, as long as it makes you feel good." While these paradigms can seem freeing and easy to embrace at first, you've probably discovered that they deliver a pretty empty, unfocused life. You quickly find out why these attitudes are not what God desires for us.

Churches are places where people—and their issues—gather. God purposely designed people to find Him through an organized, imperfect group called the church. Otherwise, we can't authentically share the truth of God, experience His love, connect with others who feel the same, and implement His way of living in an imperfect world. Yes, organized religion may be a faulty term, but organized churches really are essential to helping you find God again.

REASON #2:

I HAVE MY OWN WAY OF CONNECTING WITH GOD.

I PREFER WATCHING CHURCH SERVICES ON TV.

TV and the Internet have opened up a whole new virtual world for all of us. Do you have a screen name and friends online? Ever spent evenings chatting with your online buddies and found yourself sharing really deep stuff? Connecting is so valuable.

Watching TV-church is similar. It's great. It delivers a message that will hopefully help your life in some way. However, have you noticed that when you turn off the TV or log off your computer, there's no one there? Your situation remains the same. The house is empty for those who live alone, or filled with family who might not fully understand that gnawing hunger deep in your soul.

You can watch some really great church services on TV. If you've found one of those, good for you! But be honest–do you ever wish you could actually meet the preacher and ask him or her a question about the message? Do you ever long to process what you think God said to you, but you have no one to discuss it with? Christian chat rooms are more interactive than your TV; at least there's another lonely soul out there ready to listen to you. Just as your online buddies won't always be there when you really need to talk, TV-church can become a lesser alternative to the real thing. It won't be there for you with a kind word, a hug, or a listening ear when you come home from a really tough day or feel *so* frustrated/angry/hurt/tired/depressed or all of the above. TV is great for entertainment, but not as a spiritual and emotional lifeline.

I MEET WITH GOD IN NATURE.

You may not look for time with God electronically. Instead, you "find Him" during your times in nature: maybe while fishing at the lake, working in your garden, taking a hike, or just quietly watching the ocean at sunrise. These are all wonderful times to really appreciate God as Creator, and naturally you will feel close to Him. We *should* do this; in fact, many regular church goers may not actually do this enough. It should be a "both/and," not an "either/or," solution.

However, "church" is meant to be community. A place where you can make friends who will love you no matter what. A church friend is one who picks up the other end of the phone when you're feeling that life sucks, or a person who doesn't mind if you send them a text at 1:00 a.m. sharing how messed up you are. You can't do life alone. No one can. Spending time in nature as a form of time with God is a wonderful addition, but it's definitely not enough by itself to really help you grow.

> *"There is a God-shaped vacuum in every heart."*
>
> —BLAISE PASCAL

Did you know that the book of Acts describes the very first church? This is what they did: *"They devoted themselves to the apostles' teaching and to the fellowship, to the breaking of bread and to prayer. Everyone was filled will awe, and many wonders and miraculous signs were done by* [through] *the apostles. All the believers were together and had everything in common. Selling their possessions and goods, they gave to anyone as he had need. Every day they continued to meet together in the temple courts. They broke bread in their homes and ate together with glad and sincere hearts, praising God and enjoying the favor of all the people. And the Lord added to their number daily those who were being saved ."*[1]

Let's face it. You can't live a Christian (Christ-following) life without being part of a church, any more than a piece of charcoal can stay hot outside the fire. You need the heat of the fire to keep you going!

---

[1] Acts 2:42-47

If you have your "own way of connecting with God," it may well be hiding the "real" reason that you left the church. Perhaps you never did find the connection you needed. Maybe the church you attended didn't help you find God or the awesome power of the living Christ in your life. Watching TV-church or seeking out quiet times in nature might indicate that you long for God's Word in your life, and you still enjoy the chance to worship and pray. Take time to explore the other nine reasons. You just might discover a deeper truth about your church avoidance.

REASON #3:

I GOT TIRED OF THE CHURCH ALWAYS ASKING ME FOR MONEY.

WE SPEND HALF our lives putting down cash or swiping our pieces of plastic for absolutely everything we consume. Yet, somehow we have this notion that church should be a place where we can be entertained, cared for, taught the Word of God, and served when we have trouble–but it should all come free. True, some churches do a lousy job of the "ask," or rather, the "check-out line." But if a church is wise, it will point out that giving a part of what you have back to God (who gave it to you anyway) is actually a way to thank Him for His provision.

Many churches also state that giving an offering (a monetary contribution you give when the basket gets passed) or actively tithing (committing ten percent of your income to the church) is an act of worship for those who call that particular church "home." As a visitor, you are not expected to participate at all unless you'd like to. That should remove some of the pressure, right? Churches sometimes do discuss monetary or budget issues during a service, mostly because it's the one time everyone is there! (Kind of like calling a family meeting.) If you are not a member of the church, you're actually welcome to tune out that portion of the service.

> *"What gives me the most hope every day is God's grace; knowing that his grace is going to give me the strength for whatever I face, knowing that nothing is a surprise to God."*
>
> –RICK WARREN

Once you become an active part of a church, giving will become more natural to you as you feel the desire to give part of what has been given to you back to the church. At any rate, you should give joyfully, never out of obligation. God loves a cheerful giver. He talks about money *a lot* in the Bible, reminding us constantly that everything we have is provided by Him. Once we truly recognize this, we gladly share our resources. We also learn that taking money from the "worldly" realm and investing it into God's realm multiplies it in our own lives and in the Kingdom in ways that far exceed any investment banker's calculations! Remember the stories in the Bible you heard years ago? You know, when Jesus took the loaves of bread and a few fish and fed thousands? That could not have happened if someone didn't first offer to share what was in his lunchbox!

Jesus said: *"Do not store up for yourselves treasures on earth, where moth and rust destroy, and where thieves break in and steal. But store up for yourselves treasures in heaven, where moth and rust do not destroy, and where thieves do not break in and steal. For where your treasure is, there your heart will be also."*[2]

A church can't continue to thrive and carry out its mission without funding. Like any company or even non-profit, it needs resources to sustain it. The church is also unusual–it's the only organization that exists for the benefit of those who are not yet members! Think on that. So if the church is to take God's message to a hurting world and reach out to thousands who need Christ, the members–the family–have to help make it happen. They do this by sharing what God provides to them as individuals, so that the money can be used for God's work of building the Kingdom.

Hopefully, you will choose to visit a church again soon. After thinking about this topic, maybe you won't cringe next time someone passes the offering container.

[2] Matthew 6:19-21

REASON #4:

MY LIFE SITUATION CHANGED, AND I JUST NEVER WENT BACK.

THIS IS BY far the most common reason people leave the church. It encompasses so many life situations that it's a pretty broad statement. But, let's try to tackle some of these life-change issues that may have stopped your regular church attendance.

MOVING

Relocation is a big deal, and almost everyone goes through it at some point in their lives. When you are well-rooted in a church and then move away from it, it *is* hard to start over. By the same token, think about all the other changes you had to make. You had to learn to shop at a different store, work out at a new gym, change jobs, make new friends, and find a new hairdresser, auto repair service, drycleaner, etc. So why did finding a new church fall to the bottom of the priority list?

The longer you avoid finding a new church family, the harder it can be to find one. However, if your previous church experience was a positive one, you've probably missed it in some way. Approach the hunt for a new church home in the same way you sought out all those other places. You might have to "church shop" for several weeks before finding the right place, but that's OK.

More importantly, is this the *real* reason you haven't made time to return to church? The fact that you moved may have provided a convenient excuse to leave. In actuality, the real reason you're not in a church might be covered in one of the other sections.

RELATIONSHIP CHANGES

(MARRIAGE, CHILDREN, DIVORCE, DEATH OF A FAMILY MEMBER, ETC.)

Leaving church during *any one of these situations may have been unavoidable for logical reasons. Similar to moving, though, you probably had to make other lifestyle changes related to this disruption in your life.*

Perhaps you felt that you had to avoid the church for a while because of the trauma attached to a bad divorce. (Read Reason #10.) Maybe since you had a new baby or got married to someone who doesn't attend church, your commitment to church waned. Whatever the circumstance or type of change, you suspended your relationship with a body of believers. How has it impacted your life? Is it time to reDiscover the priority of church? Make a decision that works for you this time around, and find the right church home to welcome you back. The right church can help you manage these life changes far better than you could alone.

WORK/OTHER ACTIVITIES ON SUNDAYS

The tradition of everything shutting down on Sundays is now a distant memory. If you must participate in activities such as work, kid's sports, and others that encroach on your church schedule, it can be tough. You skip church for a few weeks, then it becomes a habit, and soon it's just no longer featured in your schedule. So what to do?

The good news is that a *lot* of churches have Saturday and/or Sunday night gatherings. Many have mid-week Bible studies and fellowship groups. Multiple options exist in today's churches, because the leadership knows how many people have to work or attend events on weekend mornings, and they're trying to meet their needs.

It's interesting that certain demands in our schedule cause us to say *yes* or *no* to other activities. Choosing how we spend our time is directly related to where our priorities lie.

A choice to make church a priority is a personal one, and only you can make it. Like any "change," it can seem easier to deal with the pain of staying the way you are, rather than the bigger pain of making a change.

For example, think about going back to the gym or starting any exercise routine. You are more likely to stay committed when the "pain" of lack of energy, obesity, or ill health is greater than the "pain" (time, energy, and physical strain) of doing the exercise. It's the same as deciding on a healthier diet, a more balanced financial plan, taking time away from work for family priority, or whatever it is that requires a reDiscover in your lifestyle.

Think through why you no longer consider church a priority in your schedule, and why you've allowed this choice to keep you away. In the long run, where is the greater level of pain?

REASON #5:

I DON'T HAVE TO GO TO CHURCH TO BE A GOOD PERSON.

THIS IS A common thought – and in some ways, you are right. There are many "good" people in this world who aren't Christian. There are also many Christians who don't go to church. Then, you have many Christians who DO go to church who are not necessarily "good" people.

Going to church is never about being good or bad. Somewhere along the way, people adopt the idea that attending church on Sundays makes a person better than someone who doesn't. The reality is that people who go to church are not necessarily "good." More often than not, they are just as messed up as anyone else and that's *why* they go to church.

> *"You can be committed to Church but not committed to Christ, but you cannot be committed to Christ and not committed to church."*
>
> –JOEL OSTEEN

When we own the fact that we make mistakes, do things that would not make God proud of us, or treat people in a less-than-gracious manner, we acknowledge that we need His help! We are not able to live the life God desires for us by going it alone.

Going to church will not make us good, but it will help us to grow. You may be a very good person, and you may live a good life. But how will you sustain your spiritual growth and development without ongoing input? It's a bit like taking a seed and putting it in soil and leaving it there. Will it grow? Probably–in fact, it may even develop into a small shrub with the help of rain, dew, and fresh air. But over time, the shrub will become stunted in its growth. The dead leaves and branches that dry out in the winter will start choking out new growth that wants to start in the spring. These new shoots have nowhere to go, so they will soon get so weak that they shrivel and die.

What if that shrub had been tended by a gardener who clipped away the dead leaves, pruned the branches, and watered, fed, and nurtured it? It would thrive and probably be in full flower every spring, constantly growing into a bigger and bigger masterpiece in the garden. Its roots would go down deep and spread wide, and it would be established and healthy. You may well be aware of some dead leaves and stunted growth in your own life. Maybe it's time to bring your shrub back to the gardener for some tending.

If you think this metaphor sounds familiar, it should. In this way, Jesus taught us about the importance of abiding (remaining) in Him. God is our gardener, Jesus is like the vine, and we are the branches. How can a branch sustain itself if it's not connected to the vine? *"Remain in me, and I will remain in you"*[3] Jesus said.

> *"Anyone who is to find Christ must first find the church. How could anyone know where Christ is and what faith is in him unless he knew where his believers are?"*
>
> —MARTIN LUTHER

The church is also known as the "bride of Christ"–that's how strongly Jesus loves and cares for it. The church is the place where we can abide and constantly be reminded of God's truth and love, both in our time with Him and in our time with others.

Maybe you never truly entered into a committed love relationship with Jesus, claiming Him as your Savior and recognizing your need for Him. Exploring what that means and understanding just how much God loves you means going back to church. Then maybe you won't just be good; you will be *better* –because God desires so much more for us than we settle for.

[3] John 15:1-17 (Read the whole section to understand his teaching.)

The process of seeking "better" over "good" is not a short-term goal. Keep in mind that God works in the "big picture," while we tend to focus on "now" or "next week." So, you may find the right church and start attending again, but after awhile (maybe a couple months) you realize nothing much has changed. You might even think, "This is just 'one more thing' I have to do each week, and I'm still the same person. I may as well just go back to my Sundays being free days again."

A great little story really teaches the lesson here: A mother takes her three-year-old son into a bakery. He spots a delicious donut at his eye-level in the display case. He wants it. He wants it bad. So he asks, pleads, bargains –only to hear "no" from his mother. It ends up that he's lying on the floor kicking and screaming…the full-blown tantrum. His mother ignores him as she speaks to the sales clerk. Finally, she calls out to him, and he looks. She leans down and opens the box of the cake she came to pick up–the one for his birthday the next day. It's the biggest, most amazing chocolate cake he's ever seen! And the mother says to her son, "I didn't want you to get that donut on the shelf because I had this for you instead."

If you went to church looking for your "donut" and never got it, did you leave forever (even throw a tantrum, perhaps) and give up? Maybe it's time to listen for the Father's voice and be patient in waiting for Him to show you what He has in store for you. I think you'll find it'll be better than any "donut" you've ever wanted.

REASON #6:

I'M TOO BUSY, AND SUNDAYS ARE MY ONLY TIME TO REST.

HAVING A DAY to rest is good; it's what God commanded (not "suggested") in the fourth commandment. God Himself invented the rhythms of life, probably because He knew that ultimately we would exist in this fast-paced, high-tech, high-stress place we call the world. By the end of the work week, you're likely brain-dead, sleep-deprived, and longing for a day of complete chill...with nothing more on the agenda than fun and a total break from the week, right?

Just as you need to recharge your mental and physical batteries on a day of rest, your spiritual battery needs charging, too. Life is just way too busy sometimes to even stop and thank God for anything. If you do pray, maybe it's those few minutes over your morning coffee when you subconsciously check off the item on your to-do list: "Shower, check. E-mail, check. Coffee, check. Pray, check. Breakfast, check..." Maybe, like church, prayer time, or even a few minutes reading your Bible has dropped off the checklist altogether. Maybe the few times you pray are when you are most stressed, and it's a cry of desperation when you realize that you are not superhuman and can't control every aspect of your life. You might also have a part of you that knows God on a basic level. You have been in His presence before, and that part of you remembers that you simply can't do life without Him.

Jesus encouraged us to abide in Him. (See Reason #5.) This includes taking time to reflect on what God has done in your life. It means making time to pray about issues weighing on your heart. Abiding is all the time, not just at certain times. But a Sabbath day is supposed to be a special time to rest and abide in Him. It's a time to worship Him, study His Word, and reflect on His truth. It's a time to enjoy the company of others who love Him, too.

> *"Church attendance is as vital to a disciple as a transfusion of rich, healthy blood to a sick man."*
>
> —DWIGHT L. MOODY

Church can become just the relaxation and time-out that your soul longs for. When you find the right church home and connect with people you learn to love, going to church will become something you look forward to and anticipate with joy, not "one more thing to do" on your schedule. Jesus promises *"rest for your soul"* and that His *"yoke is easy, and His burden is light"*[4] After all, He helps you carry it!

What if church could become something that you look forward to as much as movies, meals out with friends, your sports TV show, or your time with family? Would that make a difference? If you're wondering how the heck church could ever be like that, you just haven't found the right church yet.

"God's day of rest is a day to worship. It is not the only day to worship and not the only day to pray and praise, but it should be the day when we have to focus on God and our life in Him. It is a day to tune in again to God, to refocus and to reprioritize all that we do and are, in the light of the reality of God.... If we can take our Sabbath rest on Sunday, then giving God the first part of the first day of every week serves to remind us that He is first in our lives. Christians have always set aside time to be together. To meet with God and His people is something that serves to nourish and feed us spiritually.... Do you keep going along with the flow of the world and let it erode your relationship with God? Does God have a chance to look into your heart? Do you give Him time to do so? If not on Sunday, then when?"[5]

So rest on Sunday, and take time to rest (abide) in the One who loves you and knows you better than anyone in your life.

---

[4] Matthew 11:29-30
[5] J. John, Ten: Living the Ten Commandments in the 21st Century, (Victor Publishing, 2000)

REASON #7:

CHURCH IS BORING.

YEAH, SOME CHURCHES are boring if you put them in the same category as movies, TV, and concerts. The determination of "boring," though, is more often a reflection of our predetermined expectations and our level of engagement.

Church is not a one-way presentation where you come in to be entertained. This expectation will almost always end in a "ho-hum" result, because few churches can achieve the level of entertainment or stimulation we have come to expect. Maybe it's better to think of church as a classroom–but not like those dry, stuffy lecture halls from your college days. Bet your professor didn't allow you to stand up and sing or give you coffee at the end of the lecture!

You can also think of church as a visit with family. When you last spent time with parents or grandparents, did you go expecting to be entertained, or did you go because you *wanted* to spend time with them? A church is a gathering place where you come to *engage* with God and others.

God doesn't particularly care how cool the graphics are or what kind of beat that amazing drummer is throwing out today. He also doesn't care much about how good the dramas or video clips are, as long as they serve the purpose of delivering His really important message.

What He cares the most about is *you*. God looks into your heart and is waiting for you to open it so that He can speak to you. Going to church with an open mind and heart will take away the boredom factor in a heartbeat! When you truly catch on to the person of Jesus and the truth of God's Word, you will catch on to the amazing power and awesome *life* in His story. Church gets you excited about what God did and continues to do in the world, in people's lives–in your own life.

> *"I take the kids to church and Sunday school. They love it. I really think it's important for a child to feel that there are things that are bigger than your life out there."*
>
> —REESE WITHERSPOON

To overcome the notion that church is boring will also take a change of mindset on your part. It may also mean you'll have to shop around for a church where you can engage. Maybe your last church experience was so dull that you never contemplated trying again. Think back on that experience. Perhaps even write down what you found boring. Take a hard look at this list, and try to figure out how much of it came from your expectations and how much was truly a result of a dull church.

Create a new sense of anticipation in your heart. Try to go back to church a few times with the expectation that God will speak to you and give you some of that special "something" you've been looking for. Go there to give glory to Him and take time to thank Him, praise Him, and acknowledge Him in your life. Engage. Listen. Be patient, and leave the worldly expectations of entertainment at the door. God will rock your world if you give Him the chance!

REASON #8:

THE PEOPLE TEND TO HAVE THEIR OWN CLIQUES–I NEVER FIT IN.

IN ANY PROBLEMATIC relationship, there are always two sides to the issue. Remember, the church is a gathering place of regular people. Being a Christian doesn't make you perfect. It just makes you forgiven for being imperfect. If you have experienced a lack of "fitting in" at church, chances are you've experienced it in other settings, too. Remember the first day of anything? New job, new school, new network group? Or what about the last time you had to go to some business event and didn't know anyone? You can't really expect church to be much different.

That's because Christians are not always warm, welcoming, and friendly. It's easier to hang out with those you know, so people get into "fellowship" and may (albeit unintentionally) leave a new person out. Going to a new church with the understanding that the members mean no harm can help reduce your sense of rejection. Every person at a church was once a newcomer. It takes those first couple of connections to get things started.

On your first visit, don't expect to suddenly be welcomed and introduced to everyone. Admit it–you might not enjoy that anyway! There's some level of safety and self-protection in anonymity. But on the other hand, you may be greeted with enthusiasm. Let people greet you and welcome you, and then *you* make the next move. You might make it a goal to get to know at least one person that first visit: the person sitting next to you, or the one who served you coffee. Make the first move to introduce yourself; make eye contact and memorize the person's name. That's it. No need to force a connection.

If you find a church you think you like, take this approach every week–meet and talk to one person. By your third visit, you will know three people you can greet by name. You will probably find that by then those three people will greet you back and start to engage in longer conversations to get to know you.

Building new friendships at a church is no different than any other place in life. It takes stepping outside your comfort zone at first, and it takes effort. The church is full of all kinds of people. Chances are you will soon "click" with a few of them and be able to connect in more meaningful ways–like participating in a small group, attending a special event, or even serving on a mission project together. Before you know it, you are part of the family, too.

> *"The church is not a select circle of the immaculate, but a home where the outcast may come in. It is not a palace with gate attendants and challenging sentinels along the entrance-ways holding off at arm's-length the stranger, but rather a hospital where the broken-hearted may be healed, and where all the weary and troubled may find rest and take counsel together."*
>
> –JAMES H. AUGHEY

God desires for us to be in healthy relationships, and His greatest commandment remains, "Love God and love your neighbor as yourself." The Apostle Paul also reminded the church in Ephesus, *"Be completely humble and gentle; be patient, bearing with one another in love. Make every effort to keep the unity of the Spirit through the bond of peace."*[6]

If you do not connect at all, not with a single person, maybe it's not the right church for you. Try someplace else. "Church shopping" is harmless because this is a long-term aspect of your life that you want to rebuild. Remember, you can't do a drive-by and quit at the first bad experience. (See later chapters in this booklet for some tips on finding the right church.)

---

[6] Ephesians 4:2-3

REASON #9:

CHRISTIANS ARE JUDGMENTAL AND HYPOCRITICAL.

IF THIS IS your reason for leaving church, then we feel a special sadness and empathy for you, since you were obviously hurt at some point, or disappointed in the behavior of a church member. If you were not specifically hurt or angered, then maybe the perception is more of an internal one; you may feel Christians would judge you for something you do or are. That perception belongs more in Reason No. 10, so skip over if you need to.

As mentioned in several of the other reasons, the church is full of ordinary people with issues. In biblical times, Jesus disliked the religious leaders (Pharisees) more than any other group, even the worst of sinners. He had nothing but rebuke and stern words for the pompous leaders who tried to outdo themselves in keeping the laws and presenting themselves as "holier than thou." But Jesus had incredible patience, love, and tenderness when dealing with broken, contrite sinners...the tax collectors, the prostitutes, and even Judas, His ultimate betrayer.

You *are* going to run into judgmental and hypocritical people wherever you go, and yes, they do show up in church. If the sinners that Jesus loved allowed the Pharisees to keep them from discovering God's grace, they would have remained lost and unloved. Don't let haughty Christians keep you away either. Jesus showed us that grace, love and understanding for each other is what God desires.

Be the bigger person and don't allow a few "bad" Christians to deter you from a path toward God and His truth in your life. Realize that they exist and pray for them. Love them and acknowledge that nobody is perfect. Christians today who take a "holier than thou" stance are in desperate need of God's grace.

God can't heal a broken heart unless you give Him the pieces. Forgiveness and the saving grace of Jesus are solely dependent on *repentance*–acknowledging your sin and honestly trying to turn away from it. Bring God your mess, admit your faults, and then let Him help you work them out. Disregard any form of input from the judgmental ones, because yes, they are hypocrites. They are in as much of a mess as we all are; they just don't admit it.

> *"Going to church does not make you a Christian anymore than going to the garage makes you a car."*
>
> –DR. LAURENCE J. PETER

"So why on earth would I want to hang out with these people [Christians]*? I love Jesus with all my heart, but I find His flock annoying. During my self-exile from church, I was picky about the Christians with whom I did 'fellowship,' and often preferred the company of non-Christians. Why would I want to go to church with a bunch of people so full of crap? Because I'm even more full of crap. When God revealed that to me, I started going to church again. God had to go out of His way to remind me of this through some humbling experiences, but the proof was there all along. I just got snobby and didn't bother to look."*[7]

The church is just a gathering of all sorts of people from all walks of life. Because of that, it will include every type–even messed up, controlling and sometimes rigid and judgmental people. A wise pastor once said, *"You are always going to meet Christians that make you thankful heaven is so big."* [8]

But the right church will also include others who have a genuine desire to make a connection with you, including some really neat individuals with lots in common with you. The "church" is a whole bunch of ordinary people committed to fulfilling an extraordinary mission–building Christ's church and the Kingdom here on earth.[9] You may have to sift through lots of people and churches before you connect, but connection to people who could become lifelong friends is a real possibility–and it's what God hopes you find.

---

[7] Stephen W. Simpson, Ph.D "Why I Went Back to Church: God on the Ground," www.divinecaroline.com. Article # 22196/46212

[8] Larry Osborne, Sermon at North Coast Church, Vista, CA

[9] Matthew 18:20

REASON #10:

I DON'T THINK I'D BE WELCOME ANYMORE–I'VE DONE SOME BAD STUFF.

WELCOME! THE CHURCH is a place for sinners, not perfect people. Jesus Himself said, *"It is not the healthy who need a doctor, but the sick. I have not come to call the righteous, but sinners."* [10]

If you feel you wouldn't be welcome in church, perhaps you have been judged or criticized by Christians in the past. Or you've been made to feel "less than" because of some mistakes in your life. If that's the case, be sure to read Reason #9.

We all have "bad stuff," and we can deal with it in several different ways. We can hide it and pretend we're perfect, but this leads to a long-term, deadly growth of internal guilt and shame that festers in our hearts, often making us mean and judgmental toward others. (It also creates a tendency to hide from and avoid church, Christians, and even God.) We can share it openly at the risk of being judged and thought less of, but this leaves us vulnerable to hurt and broken friendships. Or, we can confess it to God and admit our weakness. We can pray for the grace and love of Jesus to set us free from the guilt and the pain. What choice do you think is best?

"Church is a good place for people who are full of crap. Being a Christian means that you realize you're full of crap and that you need help. Mike Yaconelli once said that church should be a place where we

[10] Mark 2:17

look at each other and say, 'What are you doing here?' None of us is good enough to be there."[11]

When Jesus was ready to hand over leadership of the church to his disciples, he chose Peter–messed up as he was–to be one of its first leaders. Peter preached the first "sermon" and was an important leader of the early church. Even today, some pastors would be impressed that his teaching resulted in 3,000 being added to the church![12] But Peter was the disciple who spent his life opening his mouth only to change feet. He was also the disciple who denied even knowing Jesus not once but *three* times (as Jesus had predicted).[13] And what about the time Peter took matters in his own hands (he was a "take-action" kind of guy) and sliced off the ear of a Roman guard?[14] If Jesus could select a guy like Peter to start the church, He could probably use you for something!

> *"It's never too late. You can't screw up so badly that God can't find something worth building in the wreckage, that life can't assert its return when it is time."*
>
> –BARBARA CRAFTON

Coming back to church will not require you to stand up and confess your bad stuff in front of a bunch of people. Heck, you don't really have to share anything with anyone. But you can find Jesus again. You can open your heart to God and let Him heal you. But to be healed and put back on track – freed of your guilt–you need to bring yourself to the hospital and then return every week for ongoing preventative spiritual care.

We're all going to mess up to varying degrees pretty much our whole lives. So choose to be forgiven, grow and learn every week, rather than trying to live on your own, licking your wounds and living in fear of being judged. God already knows anyway. So why wait? After all, His only Son died so you could live without the guilt.

---

[11] Stephen W. Simpson, Ph.D "Why I Went Back to Church: God on the Ground," www.divinecaroline.com. Article # 22196/46212

[12] Acts 2:40

[13] Matthew 26:31-35; 69-75

[14] John 18:10

WHY PEOPLE ARE COMING BACK TO CHURCH...

WE'VE TOUCHED ON many of the benefits of having a regular church life. Below is a summary of those benefits, and you may even have come up with some of your own. Think through this list, then perhaps add your own statement as to what would be better in your life if you went back to church.

> *"God loves each of us as if there were only one of us."*
>
> —ST. AUGUSTINE

TIME WITH GOD/RE-CENTERING OF THE SOUL

It's hard to live life disconnected from God. Having a regular time in church re-centers you every week and opens your heart and soul to worship. It's an opportunity to give thanks and listen to what He wants you to know about what's going on in your life.

COMMUNITY AND FRIENDSHIP WITH OTHERS

Being part of a church family creates new friendships and a whole new circle of connection apart from work or other social networks. Regular contact with others who seek out God in their lives gives you access to the power of Jesus Christ found in the body of Christ at large.

> *"Some stand on tiptoe trying to reach God to talk to him—you try too hard, friend—drop to your knees and listen to him, he'll hear you better that way."*
>
> —EVER GARRISON

SPIRITUAL GROWTH

Regular study of the Bible, hearing Bible-based teaching, and connecting with truth every week helps you grow in your understanding of God, Jesus Christ and the Holy Spirit in your life. God wants so much more for you than just the day-to-day grind, and growing spiritually contributes to a more fulfilling life.

LOVE AND FORGIVENESS

In your church family, you will receive and give a relational love not easily found elsewhere. Knowing you have forgiveness in Jesus Christ, you are better able to forgive and show grace to those around you. This makes for happier, more balanced living.

PEACE

God's peace is one that "passes all understanding." This peace creates a solid anchor deep in the soul for all the storms of life. The more time you spend knowing and experiencing God, the less time you are likely to spend feeling anxious, depressed and angry.

> *"God is the only one who can make the valley of trouble a door of hope."*
>
> —CATHERINE MARSHALL

HEALTHIER FAMILY LIFE

Marriages and families need all the help they can get these days. With the high divorce rates, and the number of troubled children as a result, people are realizing more than ever the positive impact a church life can have on a couple and the family as a whole.

> *"Of all the needs a child has, the one that must be satisfied, if there is going to be hope and a hope of wholeness, is the unshaking need for an unshakable God."*
>
> —MAYA ANGELOU (B. 1928)

According to the National Survey of Children's Health, children and youth who attend religious services weekly exhibit the fewest behavior problems, are more likely to have high-quality relationships with their parents, and are more likely to exhibit positive social behavior, including showing respect for teachers and neighbors, getting along with other children, understanding other people's feelings and trying to resolve conflicts with classmates, family or friends.

> *"The family that prays together stays together."*
>
> —AL SCALPONE

HEALTHIER LIFE BALANCE

The "self" is composed of four elements: physical (body), mental (mind), emotional (soul), and spiritual (spirit). God calls us to love Him with *all* of these. When we actively take care of ourselves in all four areas, we enjoy a balanced life and a healthier one, too. Insurance studies have actually shown that regular church attendance adds 5.7 years to your life!

Are you ready to give church another try? If so, what is the one missing element you most hope to get back into your life when you find the right church?

> *"For millions of men and women, the church has been the hospital for the soul, the school for the mind and the safe depository for moral ideas."*
>
> —GERALD R. FORD

HOW DO I GO BACK TO CHURCH?

Once you've decided to go back to church, often the confusion about exactly *how* to approach it can drive you right back into your comfort zone of excuses and procrastination. The following tips may be helpful in putting together an action plan. Whenever we make a life change, we research, plan, prepare, and seek help, and going back to church should be no different. You are more likely to have a successful experience if you plan properly.

STEP 1: WHAT AM I LOOKING FOR?

Churches are not all alike. No matter what your previous experience has been, this experience will likely be very different. Begin by defining your church criteria. Review your No.1 element from the previous page–the thing you most hope to gain from returning to church; this should become your No. 1 criteria. With that in mind, below is a list of other aspects of church you can consider. Number them from 2 – 10 in order of priority. (There are more than ten to choose from, and you could even add some of your own.)

STEP 2: SUMMARIZE YOUR CHECKLIST.

It will get confusing to have the whole list in front of you all the time, so write down your top ten criteria on an index card, five on each side. (The front of the card lists the first five priorities, the back of the card the next five.) Keep the card with you every time you visit a church during the next few weeks. If you've ever shopped for a house or an apartment rental, this is a similar exercise.

There is *no* such thing as the "perfect church," so realize that you are not likely (although it is possible) to find all ten criteria met in one place. But remember your priorities. If, for example, the fact that people your age attend is No. 3 on your list, and the church's location is No. 8 on your list–and you find a church that meets No. 3, but it's a little farther away than ideal –you could probably give it a go.

WHAT I MOST WANT TO GAIN FROM RETURNING:

CRITERIA:	PRIORITY:
Church Location	
Church Size	
Service Times	
Denomination	
The Church's Core Beliefs/Doctrines	
I Know Someone There	
Nice Building/Facilities	
Ministries and Activities Available *(to suit my needs)*	
The Pastor and His/Her teaching	
Worship Style	
Community Visibility *(i.e., the church is active in the local community)*	
People in My Age Group / Life Stage Attend There	
Ministry for Children and Youth	
Other Criteria (your own):	

STEP 3: START LISTING CHURCHES TO VISIT.

The best way to find out about churches is to ask those around you who are churchgoers. Ask people what church they attend and why they like it. Ask for the church's website address and write it down. You can also do an Internet search for churches in your area.

Look at the religious section of the newspaper; see what churches are advertising. Keep a look-out for promotional postcards, flyers, or street signs advertising churches around you.

STEP 4: RESEARCH YOUR LIST.

It may be tempting to accept an invitation from a friend to attend church with them, especially once they know you're looking. But it's important for you to do some research first to assess whether you think their church would meet your criteria. Ask your friend questions about the values and basic philosophies taught at their church. Maybe even ask what the current preaching series is about. Ask what type of music they have. Ask other questions related to your top five criteria.

When researching, surf the church's website. Although some churches are not great at keeping their websites up-to-date, many of them actually have pictures, videos, sound files of sermons and detailed information about their staff and ministries. Spend time reviewing the sites and focus on churches that appear to meet your criteria. If the core beliefs and doctrine of a church are important criteria, make sure you look for them on their website. Often they're listed under "About Us" or "Statement of Belief." If you need information that's not on the website, make a call to the church and request the information be sent to you.

STEP 5: DECIDE ON SOME CHURCHES TO VISIT.

"Shortlist" two or three churches that you'd like to visit. Of course, you can't really decide if a church will fit you until you attend it. Remember, the first visit (without a friend, that is) might be tough, but go with an open mind and heart. Pray about it and ask God to help you connect in the right place and, most importantly, hear what He has to say to you during the service. Try to make at least one connection with someone during the visit.

STEP 6: ASSESS, REVIEW, KEEP TRYING.

Be committed to attending a church at least two or three times before making a final decision. It might even take going to several churches to find just the right place. This process could continue for months, but don't get frustrated or quit. It's too important a decision to make quickly!

After every visit, carefully assess your experience in light of your criteria. Review the pros and cons of each church. After the first few visits, if you think the church is worth trying out for a few more weeks, great! If not, move to the next one. But keep trying and keep praying. God wants you back. He will help connect you to the right place eventually.

MORE TIPS ON GOING BACK TO CHURCH

You have made up your mind to visit a church this Sunday–good for you! But we know you might have some other concerns, depending on how long it's been since you have attended a service. Hopefully these tips will set you up for a great day!

WHAT TO WEAR?

Many churches practice a "business casual" or "casual" policy. Jeans are mostly accepted as are other casual clothes. Dress in what makes *you* feel comfortable, but try to show respect. Don't wear jeans that are torn or stained, and it's probably best to avoid flip-flops at first until you know just how casual the dress code is. Women should avoid revealing clothing with too much cleavage or too short a hemline.

Don't become overly anxious if you think you're under- or over-dressed. Will some people criticize/lift an eyebrow? Perhaps, and if they do, it might be an indicator that the church isn't a good fit. But remember, people are people; God is God. Who are you really there to spend time with?

WHAT TIME TO GET THERE?

Especially on a first visit, it can be embarrassing to arrive too early, like when the band is still rehearsing and people are setting up the coffee table—or too late, when things have started already and everyone notices your arrival while you search for a seat. The best rule of thumb is to get to the church ten to fifteen minutes before start time. This will allow you to find parking, figure out where the entrance is, and locate a seat where you feel most at ease.

And if you've ever had the unfortunate experience of some rigid, non-loving Christian telling you that you're in their seat, don't worry about it. Any situation where you feel "corrected" requires grace on your part; don't take it personally. It's the Christian who has the problem! Remember, the church is full of messy people, and you will meet them along the way in all churches.

MEET NEW PEOPLE–OR STAY ANONYMOUS?

This is totally your choice, as we've said before. Sometimes it's less threatening to keep a low profile on the first visit. But be polite, and when asked, introduce yourself. If someone asks if it's your first time, it's OK tell them you're "just looking!" Don't feel obliged to engage if you're not comfortable yet. Be sure to try to meet at least one other person, though. The sooner you get to know some people, the easier it will be to return, especially if you like some things about your first experience.

HOW TO ACT?

All churches have their own ways of doing things, and this can seem scary at first when you're not sure what, when or how to do these things. The best plan is to watch others around you. Regular attendees will know the routine, so follow their lead. If something seems weird or you don't understand it, just go with the flow. It will make sense eventually, and you can't be expected to know at first. But don't feel obliged to participate in any aspect of the service that makes you uncomfortable.

Remember the first day at a new school, when you didn't realize the bell meant recess? You are bound to have memories of when you felt embarrassed about being "new" at something. But it wasn't long before you were well-versed in how things were supposed to be done. Church is no different.

RESPOND TO FOLLOW-UP?

Good, organized churches will inevitably have you fill out some kind of information card. Doing this is a good thing. It helps them follow up with you via letter, e-mail, or phone call. They care about you and want to know about your experience. Don't avoid this step. Even if you hated the place, be pleasant when you make that follow-up connection.

Some follow-up teams, in their zest and enthusiasm, can be a tad persistent. But don't feel the need to make an immediate decision regarding joining a church, no matter what they say or do. Realize church people do this because they care about you, and don't let their eagerness deter you from returning if the church meets your criteria.

THE MOST IMPORTANT TIP:

Be yourself! Go with an open heart and mind, and make every effort to be responsive to God's leading in your life. He knows what will work best for you.

Thanks for taking the time to read this. The person who gave you this book cares about you. We hope you find what you're looking for and that you will rediscover all the amazing things God has in mind for you, your family and your future!

> *"If you are not as close to God as you used to be, who moved?"*
>
> —AUTHOR UNKNOWN